Let's Look at Tracks

This pictorial inquiry into the identification of animals through their tracks will sharpen observation skills in preschool and primary-grade children. A familiar animal's trail is shown, along with a textual description of the tracks to point out specific details. The reader is encouraged to use these clues to determine the animal that made the trail. Then, by turning the page, the reader sees a picture and reads about the animal that made the tracks. Animals include a squirrel, cat, mouse, dog, toad, snail, turtle, robin, sparrow, and duck.

LET'S LOOK AT
TRACKS

Written and illustrated by

ANN KIRN

G. P. PUTNAM'S SONS NEW YORK

Let's Look at Tracks

Tracks are the trails
that all animals
leave behind them.

Tracks are made
when an animal walks,
runs, crawls, or hops.

Let's look at some tracks
that you can find.

You may see the tracks
in your garden
or in a park.

This book has pictures
of those tracks.

Look at the pictures.

Try to guess
what animals
made the tracks.

Under a big oak tree,
these tracks may run
from one hole to another.

Look at the trail.

This furry animal
leaps when he runs.

The hind footprints
make tracks in front
of the paw prints.

See the five toe prints
of each hind foot.

Now look at the paw prints.

Each has only four toes.

See the prints
of the sharp claws
on all its toes.

These tracks belong to ...

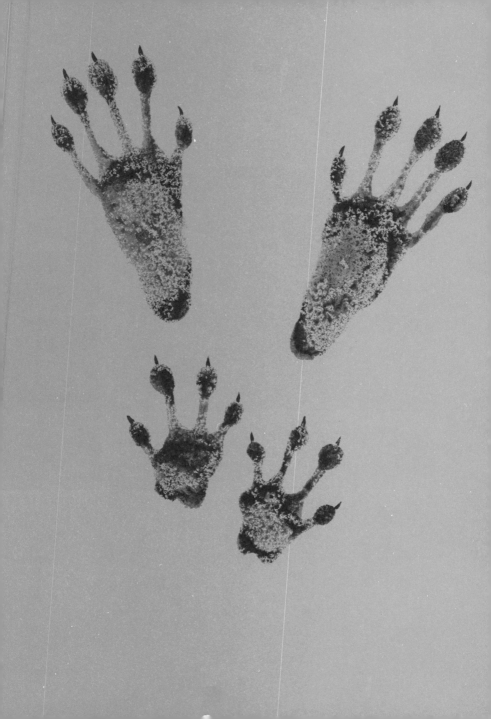

...a squirrel.

Watch the squirrel sit
as he eats his acorn.

He holds it with his paws
and gnaws it all around.

His bushy tail
curls up his back.

His tail is his blanket
when he sleeps.

It is his rudder
when he jumps.

It is his parachute
if he should fall.

He chatters away
to his friends.

The squirrels play tag
down and around the trees.

You may see these tracks
beside a garden wall.

The tracks were made
by an animal
with sharp, curved claws.

But not even one claw
shows in the footprints.

The tracks are made
by the hard pads
of toes and palms.

You cannot see tracks
of all four feet.

When the animal walks,
it puts its hind paws
in the front paw tracks.

These tracks belong to . . .

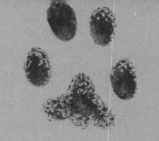

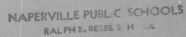

NAPERVILLE PUBLIC SCHOOLS
RALPH E. BEEBE S. H UL
DISTRICT 78
Naperville, Illinois

. . . a cat.

After her nap
on the sunny wall,
the black cat yawns.

She stretches
and arches her back.

Then she slinks
down the path,
among the red poppies.

Her night-seeing eyes
are yellow-green.

Up to the top of the tree
she climbs, like a flash.

Then she backs down
and sharpens her claws
on the rough bark.

Pressed lightly
in the damp earth
are these tiny tracks.

You may find them
where the animal looks
for its food.

This little gray animal
scampers about so fast
you would hardly see it.

It runs flat-footed,
and its small footprints
look like tiny leaves.

You can see the mark
its long tail makes
as the animal scampers.

These tracks belong to ...

14

...a mouse.

The house mouse looks out
from under the leaves
with two frightened eyes.

He cannot see very well,
but his rounded ears
will hear you on the path.

He has been stealing
red strawberries,
nibbling only the sweetest.

He spends his summer
in the garden.

But he may move
into your house
to spend his winter.

A wide path in the park
may have these tracks
printed in its dust.

The tracks were made
by an animal that yapped
as it ran along.

Look at the tracks.

The pads of the paws
with their strong claws
made deep, clear prints.

The print of the front paw
is wider than the print
of the hind paw.

Look at its trail.

These tracks belong to ...

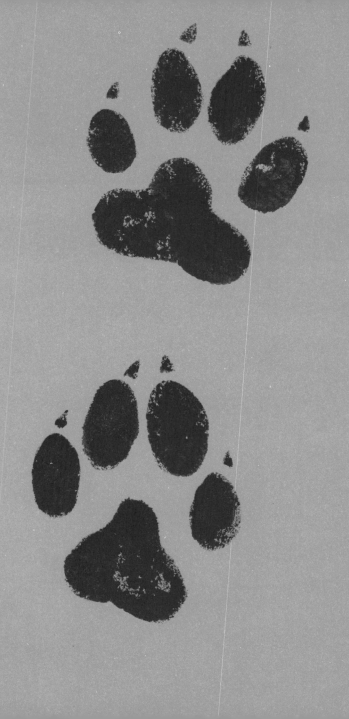

...a dog.

Down the path he comes,
sniffing a trail
with his cool, wet nose.

If you call to him,
he cocks his ears,
as his tail quivers.

Then he may spin around
and around,
chasing his tail.

He will stop to gnaw
on a juicy bone
you bring him.

He may lick your face
to thank you
for the bone.

21

In the damp earth
of a daisy bed
are these small tracks.

This little creature
hops along,
taking very short hops.

Look at its trail.

Perhaps it cannot leap far
because it is swelled up.

Look at the four toes
of each small front foot.

The front feet turn in
as the animal plops down.

The hind feet spread
to both sides
of a swelled-up tummy.

These tracks belong to ...

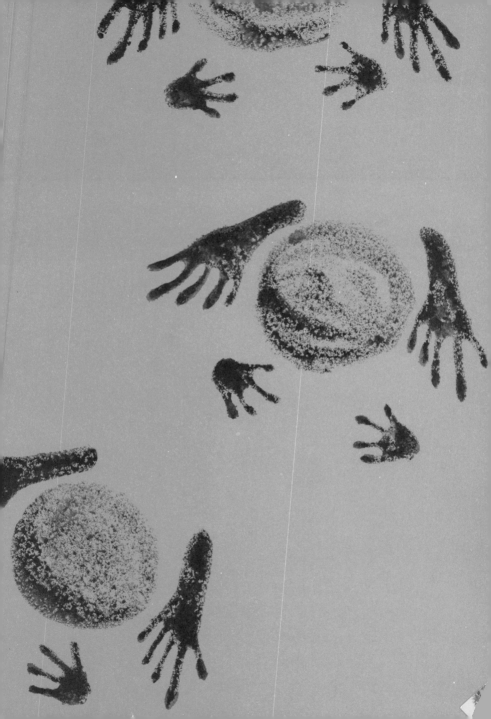

...a toad.

The squat gray toad
sits in the shade
of the white daisies.

These round flowers
seem to float
in the air above him.

He waits, watching
for a fly to buzz by.

Then he opens his mouth
and goes *gul-lup*.

He likes to bury himself
in the damp earth
to keep his skin moist.

Only his blinkng eyes
and wrinkled nose
stick out of his burrow.

On a brick path
in a garden,
you may see this trail.

It looks like a ribbon
of silver
lying on the warm bricks.

The tiny creature
who made the silvery trail
has only one foot.

It uses this slimy road
to help it get a foothold.

Look at the turns
and loops it made
as it slid slowly along.

This track belongs to...

26

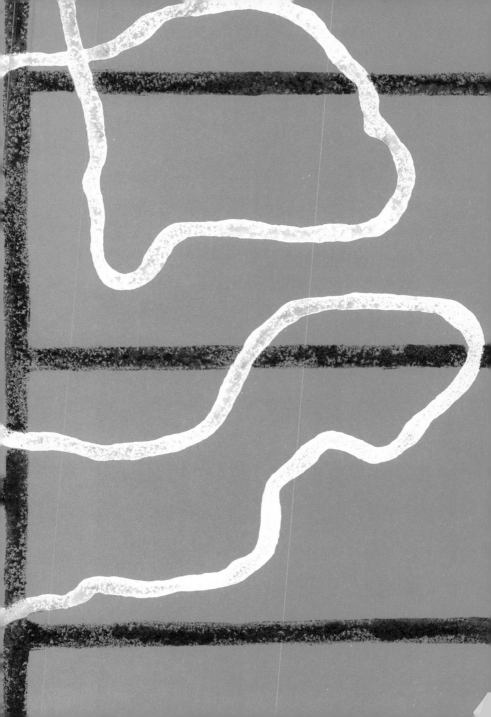

...a snail.

This garden snail
carries his tiny house
upon his back.

It is a round shell
and has stripes
of gray and white.

When he is frightened,
he pulls himself inside
and uses his foot as a door.

See him glide up the stem
of the pale-pink rose
to lunch on a juicy petal.

He feels each rosy thorn
with the tips of his eyes
on their two antennae.

You can find these tracks
in the wet earth
beside a lake in the park.

This creature can live
in water or on land.

Look at its trail.

See the print made
by its tail.

The tail makes a line,
with the paw prints
on both sides.

Each paw has five toes
with long claws.

These tracks belong to ...

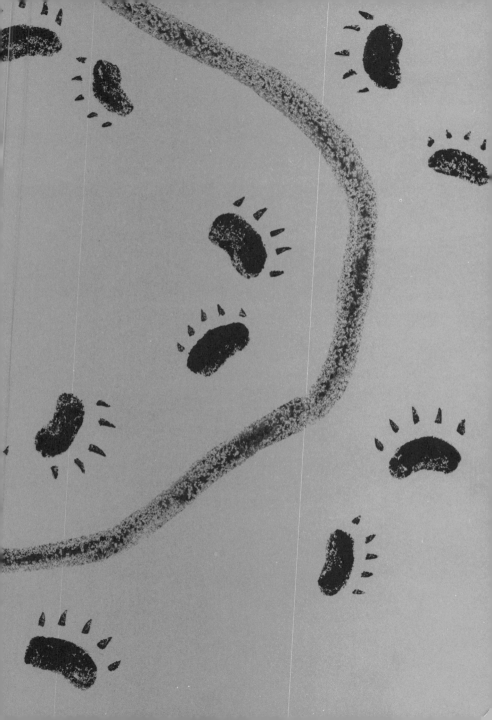

... a turtle.

The turtle lies
in the warm sunshine,
hidden in his hard shell.

Slowly he pokes out
his flat head
with its bright eyes.

Then he pokes out
his four scaly paws
and his pointed tail.

He shows his pink tongue
as he yawns with hunger.

His neck gets longer
as he walks down the path
to the pink petunias.

Look for these tracks
on the damp earth
in your garden beds.

The tracks were made
by a flying animal
that also likes the ground.

See its slender footprints
in pairs when it hops.

Then the animal runs
and puts one foot
in front of the other.

This bird hops and runs,
and hops and runs again,
with its toes turned in.

These tracks belong to . . .

34

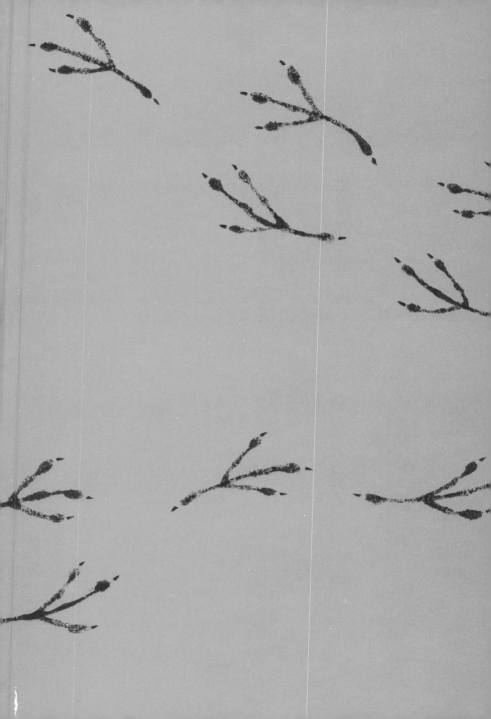

...a robin.

Robin redbreast sits
among the apple blossoms,
singing in the April air.

Then down he flits
to hop and run
in the grass.

Suddenly he stops.

He cocks his head
to listen.

His head dips down;
then up it comes.

He has a fat earthworm
held in one corner
of his beak.

Early in the morning,
when the sky is pale,
you may find these tracks.

They are bird tracks
in the damp earth
among the garden flowers.

See the three front toes
and one long back toe.

Look at the prints
made by the sharp claws.

These tracks are in pairs,
for they were made
by a perching bird.

The tracks seem to go
hop, hop, hopping along.

These tracks belong to ...

. . . a sparrow.

Many sparrows
are fluttering.

Watch them rise
and fall
in the spring sunshine.

Then they land
to scratch the ground
for seeds and insects.

They hop around,
scratching and pecking
with their little beaks.

Sparrows are so gay,
always twittering
cheep, cheep, cheep.

Did you ever go to a lake
to watch the sunset
color the water rosy?

Next time you walk down
to a lake,
look at the wet bank.

You may see these tracks.

They were made
by a waddling water bird.

Look at the web prints
between the front toes.

These webs help the bird
swim and dive.

See how the toes turn in
as the bird waddles along.

These tracks belong to . . .

... a duck.

A duck wades
in the shallow water
where reeds grow thick.

His beady eyes peer
down into the rosy water.

He is looking
for seeds or larvae
to eat for supper.

Suddenly he sees you.

He takes wing,
flying straight up
into the evening sky.

Then he quacks shrilly
out of sight.

Look at the sandy beach
or down a dusty path.

You may find these tracks.

See the two prints,
one for the left foot
and one for the right.

The palms of the prints
are long and curving.

The big toe print
is on the inside.

The four small toe prints
spread across the top.

Look at the trail.

It goes left, right,
left, right.

These tracks belong to . . .

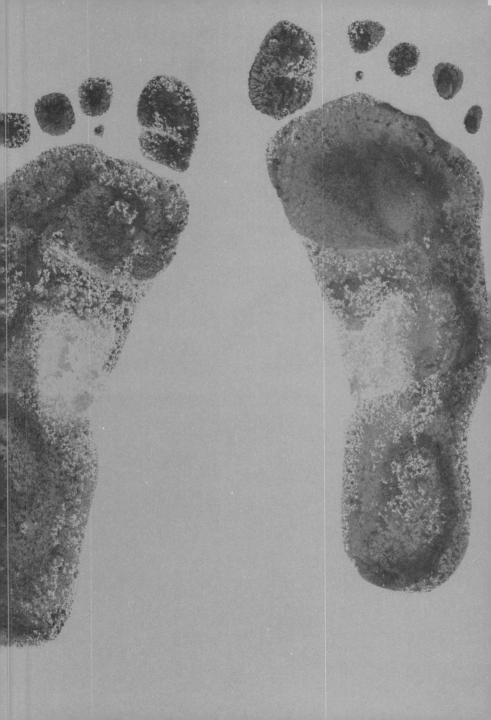

. . . a two-footed animal,

like YOU.

The Author-Artist

ANN KIRN was born in Missouri and studied art in Chicago, St. Louis, and Los Angeles. She has received a Master of Arts degree from Columbia University and for many years has taught in the Fine Arts Department of Florida State University. She makes her home in Tallahassee, Florida. Miss Kirn has written and illustrated many children's books, among them *Bamboo.*